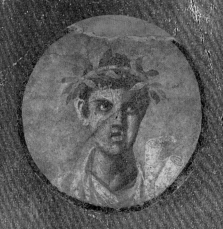

Go little book, and wish to all
Flowers in the garden, meat in the hall,
A bin of wine, a spice of wit,
A house with lawns enclosing it,
A living river by the door,
A nightingale in the sycamore.

Robert Louis Stevenson (1850-1894)

VERTUMNUM IANUMQUE, LIBER, SPECTARE VIDERIS.

Horace, *Epistles 1.20, line 1*

A GARDEN *of*
ROMAN
VERSE

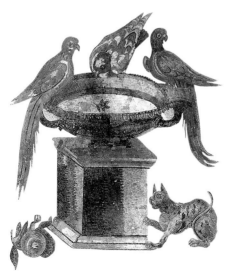

THE J. PAUL GETTY MUSEUM, LOS ANGELES

CONTENTS

CATULLUS

VIRGIL

HORACE

OVID

THE FARMER'S YEAR

The farmer cleaves the earth with his curved plough.
This is his yearlong work, thus he sustains
His homeland, thus his little grandchildren,
His herds and trusty bullocks. Never a pause!
The seasons teem with fruits, the young of flocks,
Or sheaves of Ceres' corn; they load the furrows
And burst the barns with produce. Then, come winter,
The olive-press is busy; sleek with acorns
The pigs come home; the arbutes in the woods
Give berries; autumn sheds its varied windfalls;
And high on sunny terraces of rock
The mellow vintage ripens.

L.P. Wilkinson (1907-1985)

AGRICOLA INCURVO TERRAM DIMOVIT ARATRO:
HINC ANNI LABOR. HINC PATRIAM PARVOSQUE NEPOTES
SUSTINET. HINC ARMENTA BOUM MERITOSQUE IUVENCOS.
NEC REQUIES. QUIN AUT POMIS EXUBERET ANNUS
AUT FETU PECORUM AUT CEREALIS MERGITE CULMI.
PROVENTUQUE ONERET SULCOS ATQUE HORREA VINCAT.
VENIT HIEMS: TERITUR SICYONIA BACA TRAPETIS.
GLANDE SUES LAETI REDEUNT. DANT ARBUTA SILVAE:
ET VARIOS PONIT FETUS AUTUMNUS. ET ALTE
MITIS IN APRICIS COQUITUR VINDEMIA SAXIS.

Virgil, *Georgics 2, lines 513-522*

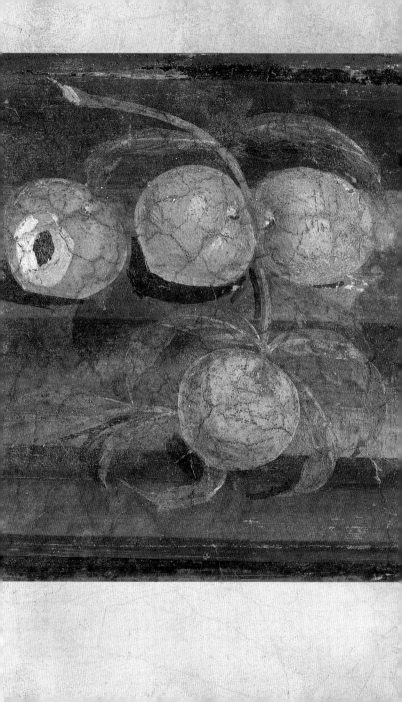

VIRGIL INTRODUCES
HIS HERO, AENEAS

Arms, and the man I sing; who, forced by fate,
And haughty Juno's unrelenting hate,
Expelled and exiled, left the Trojan shore:
Long labours, both by sea and land he bore,
And in the doubtful war, before he won
The Latian realm, and built the destined town:
His banished gods restored to rites divine,
And settled sure succession in his line:
From whence the race of Alban fathers come,
And the long glories of majestic Rome.

John Dryden (1631-1700)

ARMA VIRUMQUE CANO, TROIAE QUI PRIMUS AB ORIS
ITALIAM FATO PROFUGUS LAVINIAQUE VENIT
LITORA, MULTUM ILLE ET TERRIS IACTATUS ET ALTO
VI SUPERUM, SAEVAE MEMOREM IUNONIS OB IRAM,
MULTA QUOQUE ET BELLO PASSUS, DUM CONDERET URBEM
INFERRETQUE DEOS LATIO; GENUS UNDE LATINUM
ALBANIQUE PATRES ATQUE ALTAE MOENIA ROMAE.

Virgil, *Aeneid 1, lines 1-7*

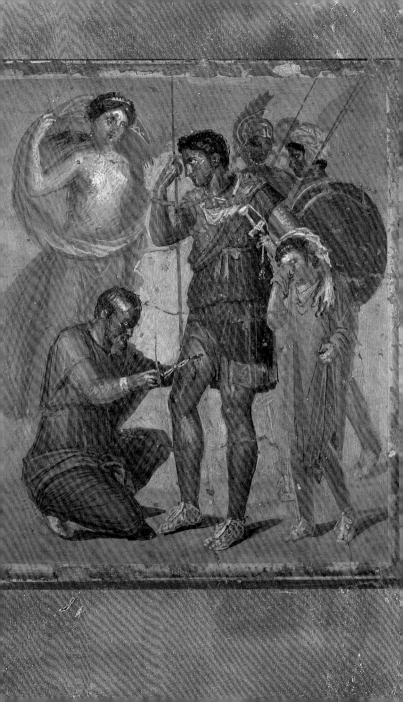

SAPPHO'S LETTER

Return fair youth, return, and bring along
Joy to my soul, and vigour to my song:
Absent from thee, the poet's flame expires;
But ah! how fiercely burn the lover's fires?
Gods! can no prayers, no sighs, no numbers move
One savage heart, or teach it how to love?
The winds my prayers, my sighs, my numbers bear,
The flying winds have lost them all in air!
Oh when, alas! shall more auspicious gales
To these fond eyes restore thy welcome sails?
If you return – ah why these long delays?
Poor Sappho dies while careless Phaon stays.

Alexander Pope (1688-1744)

EFFICITE UT REDEAT: VATES QUOQUE VESTRA REDIBIT.
INGENIO VIRES ILLE DAT. ILLE RAPIT.
ECQUID AGO PRECIBUS. PECTUSVE AGRESTE MOVETUR?
AN RIGET. ET ZEPHYRI VERBA CADUCA FERUNT?
QUI MEA VERBA FERUNT. VELLEM TUA VELA REFERRENT:
HOC TE. SI SAPERES. LENTE. DECEBAT OPUS.
SIVE REDIS. PUPPIQUE TUAE VOTIVA PARANTUR
MUNERA. QUID LACERAS PECTORA NOSTRA MORA?

Ovid, *Heroides 15, Sappho to Phaon,*
lines 205-212

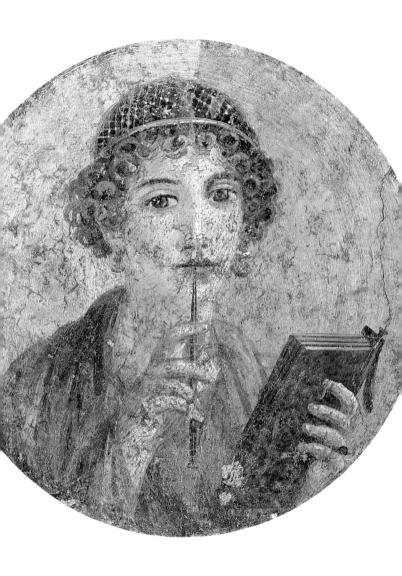

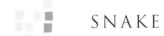

SNAKE

In fair Calabria's woods, a snake is bred,
With curling crest, and with advancing head:
Waving he rolls, and makes a winding track;
His belly spotted, burnished is his back:
While springs are broken, while the southern air
And dropping heavens, the moistened earth repair,
He lives on standing lakes, and trembling bogs,
And fills his maw with fish, or with loquacious frogs.

John Dryden (1631-1700)

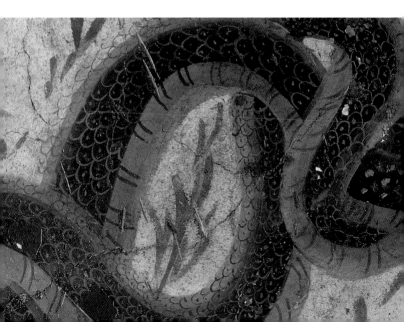

EST ETIAM ILLE MALUS CALABRIS IN SALTIBUS ANGUIS.

SQUAMEA CONVOLVENS SUBLATO PECTORE TERGA

ATQUE NOTIS LONGAM MACULOSUS GRANDIBUS ALVUM.

QUI. DUM AMNES ULLI RUMPUNTUR FONTIBUS ET DUM

VERE MADENT UDO TERRAE AC PLUVIALIBUS AUSTRIS.

STAGNA COLIT RIPISQUE HABITANS HIC PISCIBUS ATRAM

IMPROBUS INGLUVIEM RANISQUE LOQUACIBUS EXPLET.

Virgil, *Georgics 3, lines 425-431*

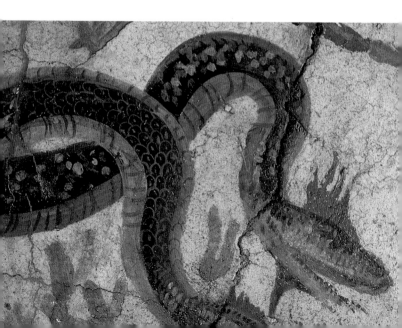

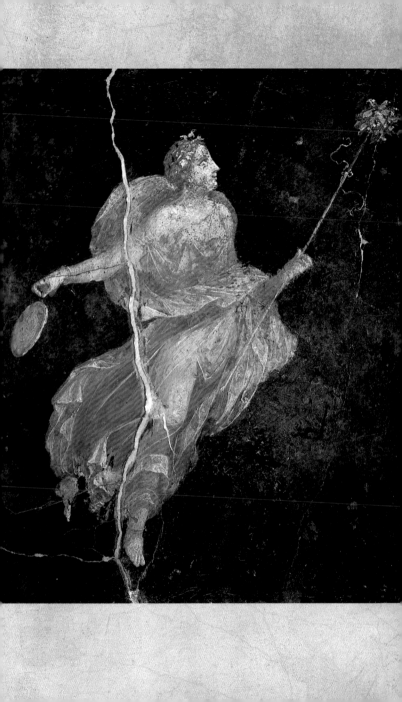

RUMOUR SPREADS

The loud report through Lybian cities goes;
Fame, the great ill, from small beginnings grows.
Swift from the first; and every moment brings
New vigour to her flights, new pinions to her wings.
Soon grows the pygmy to gigantic size;
Her feet on earth, her forehead in the skies:
Enraged against the gods, revengeful Earth
Produced her last of the Titanian birth.

John Dryden (1631-1700)

EXTEMPLO LIBYAE MAGNAS IT FAMA PER URBES.
FAMA. MALUM QUA NON ALIUD VELOCIUS ULLUM:
MOBILITATE VIGET VIRISQUE ADQUIRIT EUNDO.
PARVA METU PRIMO. MOX SESE ATTOLLIT IN AURAS
INGREDITURQUE SOLO ET CAPUT INTER NUBILA CONDIT.
ILLAM TERRA PARENS IRA INRITATA DEORUM
EXTREMAM. UT PERHIBENT. COEO ENCELADOQUE SOROREM
PROGENUIT.

Virgil, *Aeneid 4, lines 173-180*

IN PRAISE OF THE COUNTRYSIDE

See what delights in sylvan scenes appear!
Descending gods have found Elysium here.
In woods bright Venus with Adonis strayed,
And chaste Diana haunts the forest shade.
Come, lovely nymph, and bless the silent hours,
When swains from shearing seek their nightly bowers;
When weary reapers quit the sultry field,
And crowned with corn, their thanks to Ceres yield.

Alexander Pope (1688-1744)

HIC TAMEN HANC MECUM POTERAS REQUIESCERE NOCTEM
FRONDE SUPER VIRIDI: SUNT NOBIS MITIA POMA.
CASTANEAE MOLLES ET PRESSI COPIA LACTIS:
ET IAM SUMMA PROCUL VILLARUM CULMINA FUMANT
MAIORESQUE CADUNT ALTIS DE MONTIBUS UMBRAE.

Virgil, *Eclogue 1, lines 79-83*

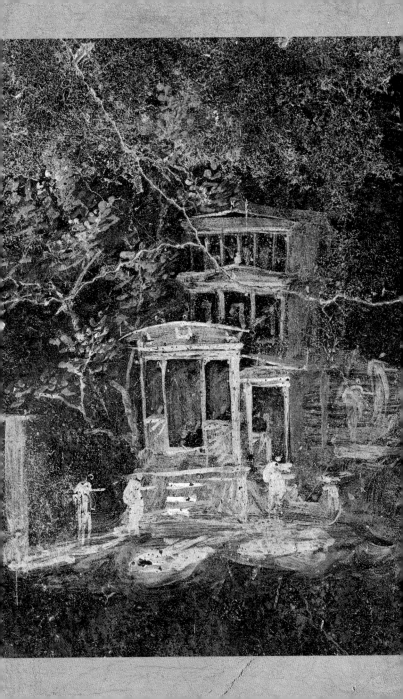

JEALOUSY

Equal to Jove, that youth must be,
Greater than Jove, he seems to me,
Who, free from jealousy's alarms,
Securely, views thy matchless charms;
That cheek, which ever dimpling glows,
That mouth, from whence such music flows,
To him, alike, are always known,
Reserved for him, and him alone.
Ah! Lesbia! though 'tis death to me,
I cannot choose but look on thee.

George Gordon, Lord Byron (1788-1824)

ILLE MI PAR ESSE DEO VIDETUR.
ILLE. SI FAS EST. SUPERARE DIVOS.
QUI SEDENS ADVERSUS IDENTIDEM TE
SPECTAT ET AUDIT

DULCE RIDENTEM. MISERO QUOD OMNIS
ERIPIT SENSUS MIHI: NAM SIMUL TE.
LESBIA. ASPEXI. NIHIL EST SUPER MI
VOCIS IN ORE

LINGUA SED TORPET. TENUIS SUB ARTUS
FLAMMA DEMANAT. SONITU SUOPTE
TINTINANT AURES. GEMINA TEGUNTUR
LUMINA NOCTE.

Catullus, *Poem 51*

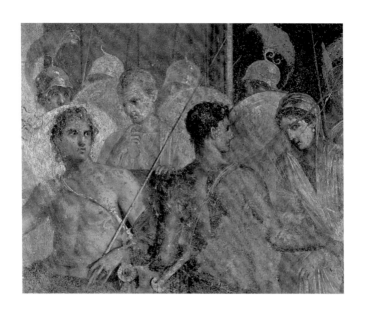

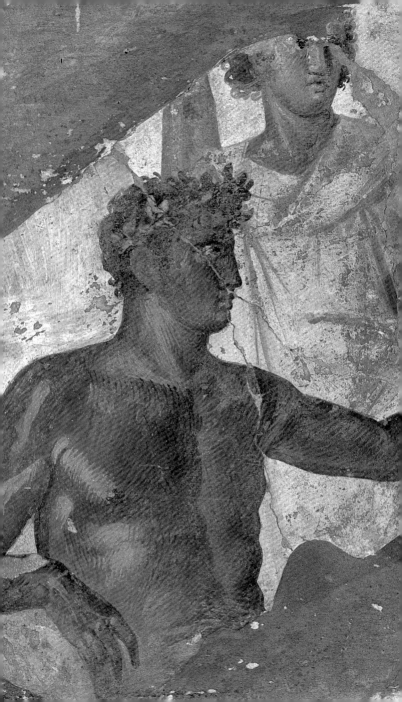

HAPPY THE MAN

Happy the man, and happy he alone,

    He, who can call today his own:

    He, who secure within, can say

Tomorrow do thy worst, for I have lived today.

    Be fair, or foul, or rain, or shine,

The joys I have possessed, in spite of fate are mine.

    Not heaven itself upon the past has power;

But what has been, has been, and I have had my hour.

John Dryden (1631-1700)

ILLE POTENS SUI

LAETUSQUE DEGET, CUI LICET IN DIEM

DIXISSE "VIXI: CRAS VEL ATRA

NUBE POLUM PATER OCCUPATO

VEL SOLE PURO: NON TAMEN IRRITUM,

QUODEUMQUE RETRO EST, EFFICIET, NEQUE

DIFFINGET INFECTUMQUE REDDET,

QUOD FUGIENS SEMEL HORA VEXIT.

Horace, *Odes 3.29, lines 41-48*

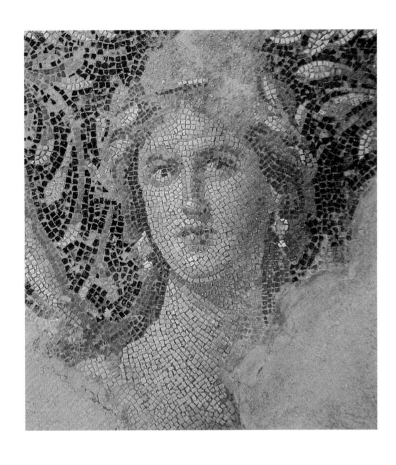

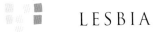

LESBIA

Lesbia for ever on me rails,
To talk of me she never fails.
Now, hang me, but for all her art,
I find, that I have gained her heart.
My proof is thus: I plainly see,
The case is just the same with me;
I curse her every hour sincerely,
Yet, hang me, but I love her dearly.

Jonathan Swift (1667-1745)

LESBIA MI DICIT SEMPER MALE NEC TACET UMQUAM
DE ME: LESBIA ME DISPEREAM NISI AMAT.
QUO SIGNO? QUIA SUNT TOTIDEM MEA: DEPRECOR ILLAM
ASSIDUE. VERUM DISPEREAM NISI AMO.

Catullus, *Poem 92*

ELEGY

Ye cupids, droop each little head,
Nor let your wings with joy be spread,
My Lesbia's favourite bird is dead,
    Whom dearer than her eyes she loved:
For he was gentle, and so true,
Obedient to her call he flew,
No tear, no wild alarm he knew,
    But lightly o'er her bosom moved.

George Gordon, Lord Byron (1788-1824)

LUGETE. O VENERES CUPIDINESQUE.
ET QUANTUMST HOMINUM VENUSTIORUM.
PASSER MORTUUS EST MEAE PUELLAE.
PASSER. DELICIAE MEAE PUELLAE.
QUEM PLUS ILLA OCULIS SUIS AMABAT:
NAM MELLITUS ERAT SUAMQUE NORAT
IPSAM TAM BENE QUAM PUELLA MATREM:
NEC SESE A GREMIO ILLIUS MOVEBAT.

Catullus, *Poem 3, lines 1-8*

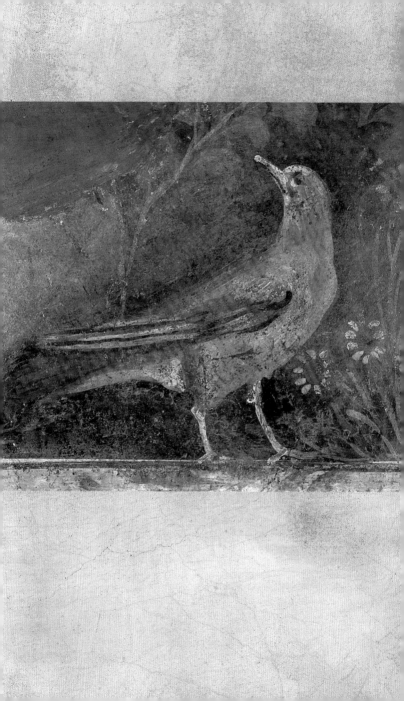

HAIL AND FAREWELL

By ways remote and distant waters sped,
Brother, to thy sad grave-side am I come,
That I may give the last gifts to the dead,
And vainly parley with thine ashes dumb:
Since she who now bestows and now denies
Hath ta'en thee, hapless brother, from mine eyes.

But lo! These gifts, the heirlooms of past years,
Are made sad things to grace thy coffin shell,
Take them, all drenchèd with a brother's tears,
And, brother, for all time, hail and farewell!

Aubrey Beardsley (1872-1898)

MULTAS PER GENTES ET MULTA PER AEQUORA VECTUS
ADVENIO HAS MISERAS. FRATER. AD INFERIAS.
UT TE POSTREMO DONAREM MUNERE MORTIS
ET MUTAM NEQUIQUAM ALLOQUERER CINEREM.
QUANDOQUIDEM FORTUNA MIHI TETE ABSTULIT IPSUM.
HEU MISER INDIGNE FRATER ADEMPTE MIHI.
NUNC TAMEN INTEREA HAEC. PRISCO QUAE MORE PARENTUM
TRADITA SUNT TRISTI MUNERE AD INFERIAS.
ACCIPE FRATERNO MULTUM MANANTIA FLETU.
ATQUE IN PERPETUUM. FRATER. AVE ATQUE VALE.

Catullus, *Poem 101*

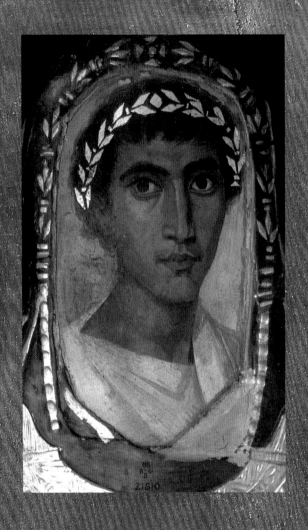

WHERE-E'ER YOU WALK

Some god conduct you to these blissful seats,
The mossy fountains and the green retreats!
Where-e'er you walk, cool gales shall fan the glade,
Trees, where you sit, shall crowd into a shade,
Where-e'er you tread, the blushing flowers shall rise,
And all things flourish where you turn your eyes.

Alexander Pope (1688-1744)

MUSCOSI FONTES ET SOMNO MOLLIOR HERBA.
ET QUAE VOS RARA VIRIDIS TEGIT ARBUTUS UMBRA.

Virgil, *Eclogue 7, lines 45-46*

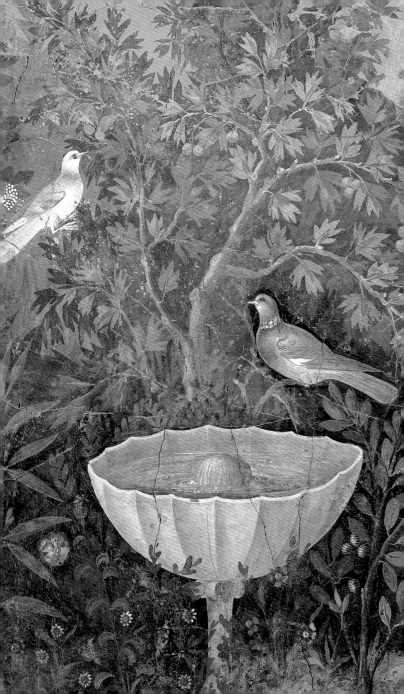

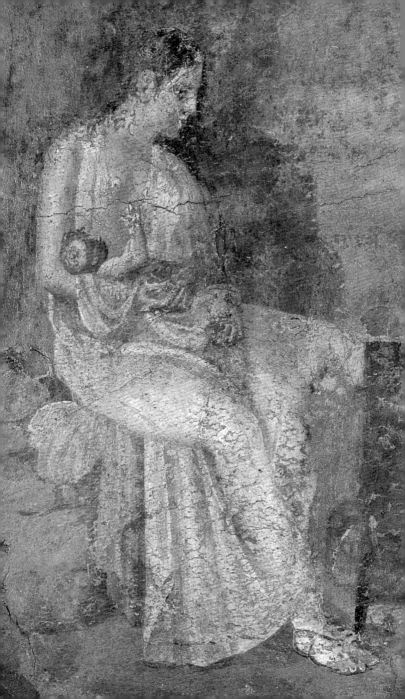

BIRTH AND DEATH

Then to be bor'n, is to begin to be
Some other thing we were not formerly;
And what we call to die, is not to appear,
Or be the thing that formerly we were.
Those very elements which we partake,
Alive, when dead some other bodies make:
Translated grow, have sense, or can discourse,
But Death on deathless substance has no force.

John Dryden (1631-1700)

NASCIQUE VOCATUR
INCIPERE ESSE ALIUD. QUAM QUOD FUIT ANTE. MORIQUE
DESINERE ILLUD IDEM. CUM SINT HUC FORSITAN ILLA.
HAEC TRANSLATA ILLUC. SUMMA TAMEN OMNIA CONSTANT.

Ovid, *Metamorphoses 15, lines 255-258*

IN MY FASHION

Last night, ah, yesternight, betwixt her lips and mine
There fell thy shadow, Cynara! thy breath was shed
Upon my soul between the kisses and the wine;
And I was desolate and sick of an old passion,
    Yea, I was desolate and bowed my head:
I have been faithful to thee, Cynara! in my fashion.

All night upon mine heart I felt her warm heart beat,
Night-long within mine arms in love and sleep she lay;
Surely the kisses of her bought red mouth were sweet;
But I was desolate and sick of an old passion,
    When I awoke and found the dawn was gray:
I have been faithful to thee, Cynara! in my fashion.

Ernest Dowson (1867-1900)

NON SUM QUALIS ERAM BONAE
SUB REGNO CYNARAE.

Horace, *Odes 4.1, lines 3-4*

.

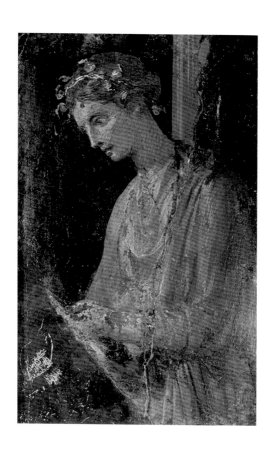

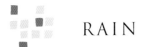

RAIN

Wet weather seldom hurts the most unwise,
So plain the signs, such prophets are the skies:
The wary crane foresees it first, and sails
Above the storm, and leaves the lowly vales:
The cow looks up, and from afar can find
The change of heaven, and snuffs it in the wind.
The swallow skims the river's watery face,
The frogs renew the croaks of their loquacious race.

John Dryden (1631-1700)

NUMQUAM IMPRUDENTIBUS IMBER
OBFUIT: AUT ILLUM SURGENTEM VALLIBUS IMIS
AERIAE FUGERE GRUES. AUT BUCULA CAELUM
SUSPICIENS PATULIS CAPTAVIT NARIBUS AURAS.
AUT ARGUTA LACUS CIRCUMVOLITAVIT HIRUNDO
ET VETEREM IN LIMO RANAE CECINERE QUERELAM.

Virgil, *Georgics 1, lines 373-378*

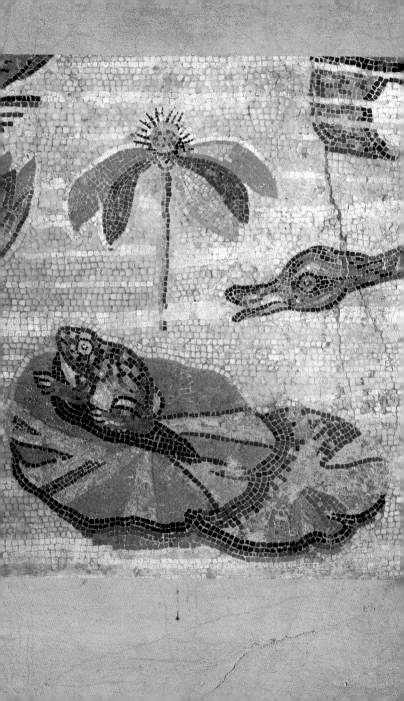

THE PAIN OF LOVE

I hate and love, wouldst thou the reason know?
I know not, but I burn, and feel it so.

Richard Lovelace (1618-1657/1658)

ODI ET AMO. QUARE ID FACIAM. FORTASSE REQUIRIS.
NESCIO. SED FIERI SENTIO ET EXCRUCIOR.

Catullus, *Poem 85*

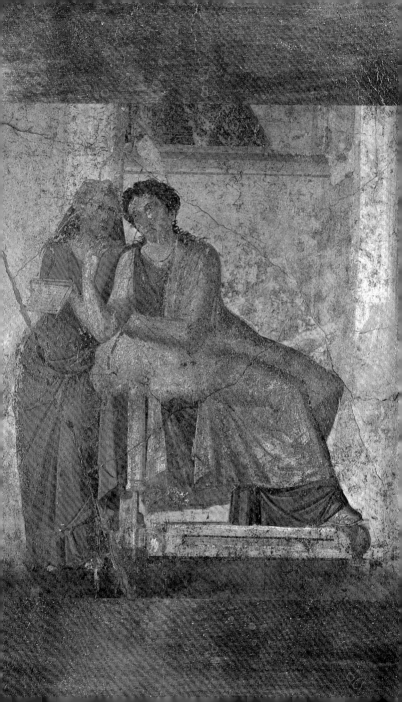

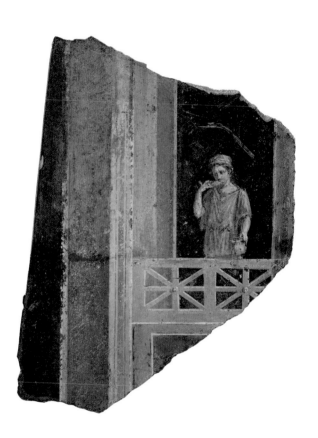

THE END OF PASSION

The bloods and bucks of this lewd town
   No longer shake your windows down
    With knocking;
Your door stands still, no more you hear
'I die for you, O Lydia dear',
    Love's god your slumbers rocking.

       The Young Gentlemen of Mr Rule's Academy
       at Islington (published 1766)

    PARCIUS IUNCTAS QUATIUNT FENESTRAS
    ICTIBUS CREBRIS IUVENES PROTERVI,
    NEC TIBI SOMNOS ADIMUNT, AMATQUE
        IANUA LIMEN,
    QUAE PRIUS MULTUM FACILIS MOVEBAT
    CARDINES: AUDIS MINUS ET MINUS IAM:
        'ME TUO LONGAS PEREUNTE NOCTES,
        LYDIA, DORMIS?'

       Horace, *Odes 1.25, lines 1-8*

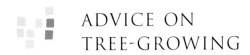

ADVICE ON
TREE-GROWING

First, different trees have diverse birth assigned;
For some lack no compulsion of mankind,
But spring spontaneously in every nook,
Peopling the meadows and the mazy brook;
Thus osiers lithe, and brooms that gently play,
The poplar, and the willow silver-grey.

    And some arise from seed themselves have shed;
For so the chestnut rears its lofty head,
The bay-oak, towering monarch of the wood,
And oaks with Grecian oracles endued.

R.D. Blackmore (1825-1900)

PRINCIPIO ARBORIBUS VARIA EST NATURA CREANDIS.
NAMQUE ALIAE NULLIS HOMINUM COGENTIBUS IPSAE
SPONTE SUA VENIUNT CAMPOSQUE ET FLUMINA LATE
CURVA TENENT. UT MOLLE SILER LENTAEQUE GENISTAE.
POPULUS ET GLAUCA CANENTIA FRONDE SALICTA:
PARS AUTEM POSITO SURGUNT DE SEMINE. UT ALTAE
CASTANEAE. NEMORUMQUE IOVI QUAE MAXIMA FRONDET
AESCULUS. ATQUE HABITAE GRAIS ORACULA QUERCUS.

Virgil, *Georgics 2, lines 9-16*

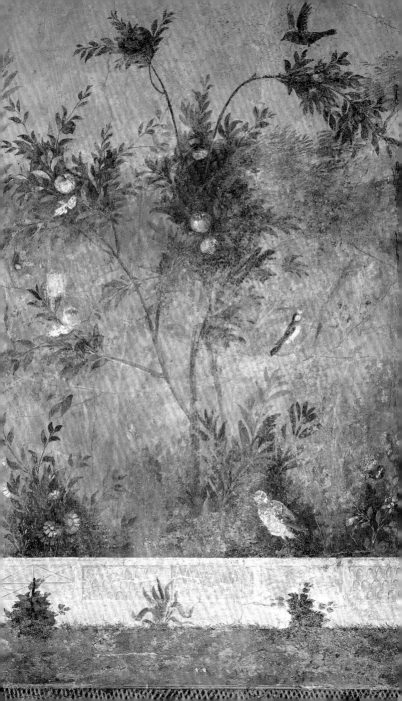

TOWN VERSUS COUNTRYSIDE

Does art through pipes, a purer water bring
Than that which nature strains into a spring?
Can all your tapestries, or your pictures show
More beauties than in herbs and flowers do grow?
Fountains and trees our wearied pride do please,
Even in the midst of gilded palaces.
And in your towns that prospect gives delight,
Which opens round the country to our sight.

Abraham Cowley (1618-1667)

PURIOR IN VICIS AQUA TENDIT RUMPERE PLUMBUM.
QUAM QUAE PER PRONUM TREPIDAT CUM MURMURE RIVUM?
NEMPE INTER VARIAS NUTRITUR SILVA COLUMNAS.
LAUDATURQUE DOMUS LONGOS QUAE PROSPICIT AGROS.
NATURAM EXPELLAS FURCA. TAMEN USQUE RECURRET.
ET MALA PERRUMPET FURTIM FASTIDIA VICTRIX.

Horace, *Epistle 1.10, lines 20-25*

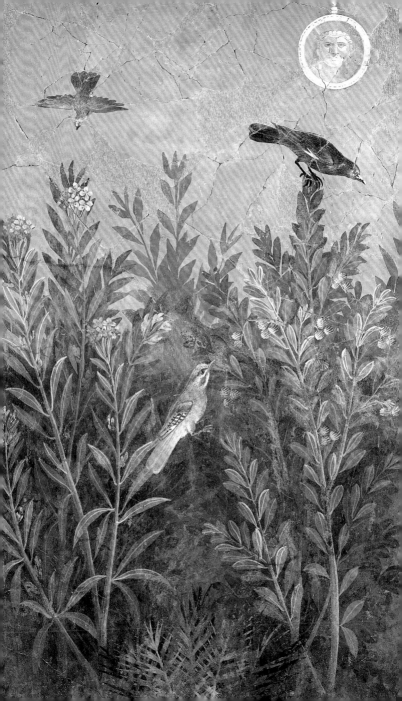

A REMEDY FOR LOVE

Although thy heart with fire like Etna flame,

Let not thy mistress once perceive the same;

Smother thy passions, and let not thy face

Tell thy mind's secrets, while she is in place:

Thy heart being stormy, let thy face be clear,

Nor let love's fire by smoke of sighs appear.

Dissemble long, till thy dissembling breed

Such use, as thou art out of love indeed.

Sir Thomas Overbury (1581-1613)

QUAMVIS INFELIX MEDIA TORREBERIS AETNA:

FRIGIDIOR GLACIE FAC VIDEARE TUAE.

ET SANUM SIMULA: NE SIQUID FORTE DOLEBIS.

SENTIAT. ET RIDE. CUM TIBI FLENDUS ERIS.

NON EGO TE IUBEO MEDIAS ABRUMPERE CURAS:

NON SUNT IMPERII TAM FERA IUSSA MEI.

QUOD NON ES. SIMULA: POSITOSQUE IMITARE FURORES:

SIC FACIES VERE. QUOD MEDITATUS ERIS.

Ovid, *The Remedies for Love*, lines 491-498

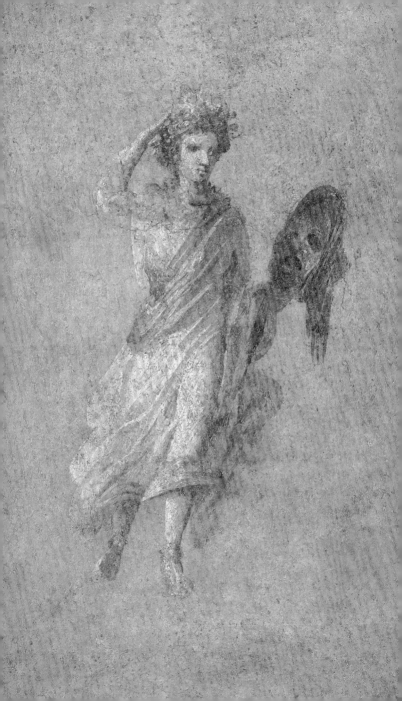

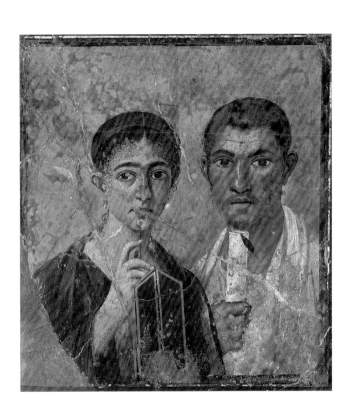

LIVING AND LOVING

Be not ever pondering
Over what the morn may bring;
Whether it be joy or pain,
Wisely count it all as gain;
And, while age forbears to shed
Snows, or sorrows o'er thy head,
Do not scorn the dancers' feet,
Nor thy lover's dear retreat.

Branwell Brontë (1817-1848)

Horace, *Odes 1.9, lines 13-18*

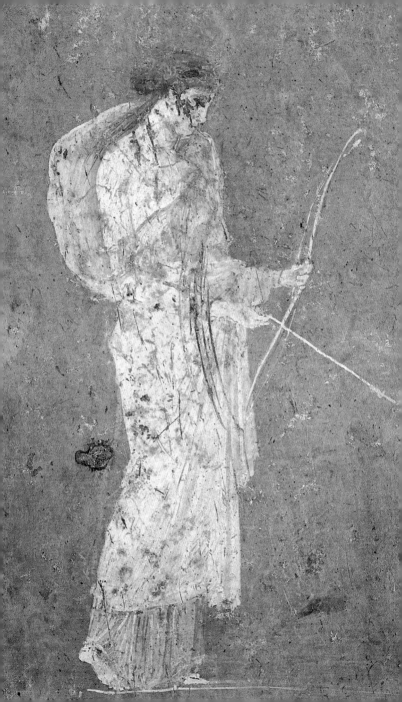

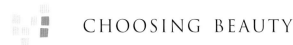

CHOOSING BEAUTY

Quintia is beautiful, many will tell you: to me
She is white, she is straight, she is tall: to all this
    I agree,
But does this make her beautiful? Though she
    be found without fault,
Can you find in the whole of her body the least
    pinch of salt?
But Lesbia is beautiful: hers is the secret alone
To steal from all beauty its beauty, and make it
    her own.

Arthur Symons (1865-1945)

QUINTIA FORMOSAST MULTIS: MIHI CANDIDA. LONGA.
RECTAST. HAEC EGO SIC SINGULA CONFITEOR.
TOTUM ILLUD FORMOSA NEGO: NAM NULLA VENUSTAS.
NULLA IN TAM MAGNOST CORPORE MICA SALIS.
LESBIA FORMOSAST. QUAE CUM PULCHERRIMA TOTAST.
TUM OMNIBUS UNA OMNIS SURRIPUIT VENERES.

Catullus, *Poem 86*

TO PYRRHA

Say what slim youth, with moist perfumes
    Bedaubed, now courts thy fond embrace,
There, where the frequent rose-tree blooms,
    And makes the grot so sweet a place?
Pyrrha, for whom with such an air
Do you bind back your golden hair?

Christopher Smart (1722-1771)

QUIS MULTA GRACILIS TE PUER IN ROSA
PERFUSUS LIQUIDIS URGET ODORIBUS
GRATO. PYRRHA. SUB ANTRO?
    CUI FLAVAM RELIGAS COMAM
SIMPLEX MUNDITIIS?

Horace, *Odes 1.5, lines 1-5*

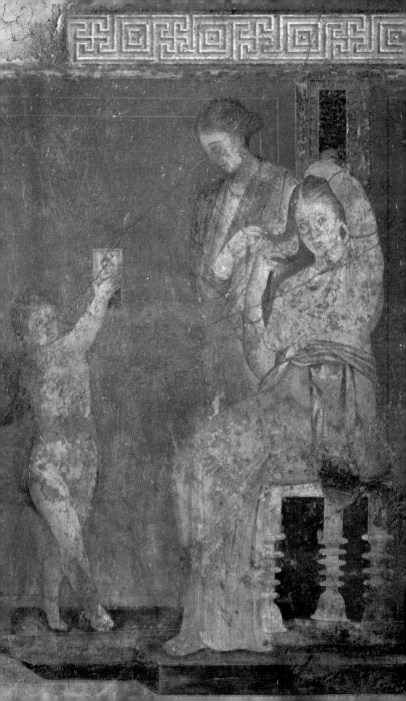

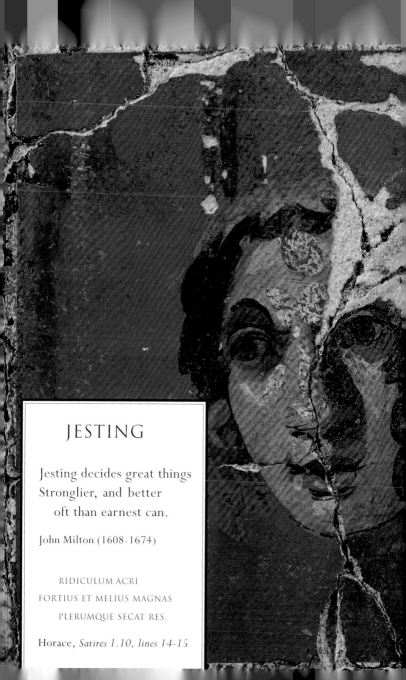

JESTING

Jesting decides great things
Stronglier, and better
oft than earnest can.

John Milton (1608-1674)

RIDICULUM ACRI
FORTIUS ET MELIUS MAGNAS
PLERUMQUE SECAT RES.

Horace, *Satires 1.10, lines 14-15*

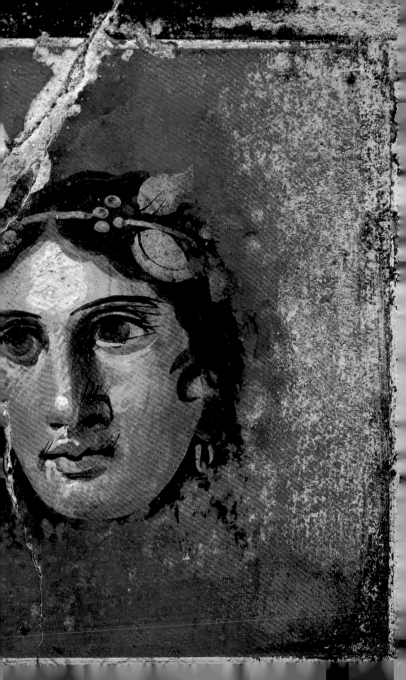

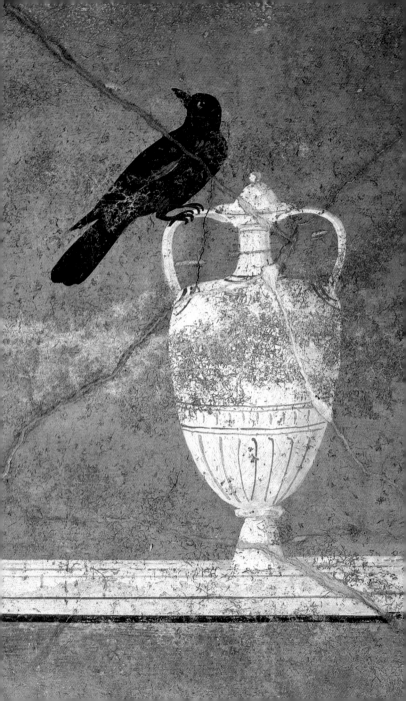

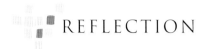 REFLECTION

The sun may set and rise:
But we contrariwise
Sleep after our short light
One everlasting night.

Sir Walter Raleigh (1554-1618)

SOLES OCCIDERE ET REDIRE POSSUNT:
NOBIS. CUM SEMEL OCCIDIT BREVIS LUX.
NOX EST PERPETUA UNA DORMIENDA.

Catullus, *Poem 5, lines 4-6*

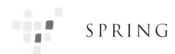

SPRING

Sharp winter now dissolved, the linnets sing,
The grateful breath of pleasing Zephyrs bring
The welcome joys of long desired spring.

The galleys now for open sea prepare,
The herds forsake their stalls for balmy air,
The fields adorned with green the approaching
    sun declare.

In shining nights the charming Venus leads
Her troop of Graces, and her lovely maids
Who gaily trip the ground in myrtle shades.

             Lady Mary Wortley Montagu (1689-1762)

SOLVITUR ACRIS HIEMS GRATA VICE VERIS ET FAVONI,
    TRAHUNTQUE SICCAS MACHINAE CARINAS.
AC NEQUE IAM STABULIS GAUDET PECUS AUT ARATOR IGNI;
    NEC PRATA CANIS ALBICANT PRUINIS.
IAM CYTHEREA CHOROS DUCIT VENUS IMMINENTE LUNA,
    IUNCTAEQUE NYMPHIS GRATIAE DECENTES
ALTERNO TERRAM QUATIUNT PEDE.

        Horace, *Odes 1.4, lines 1-7*

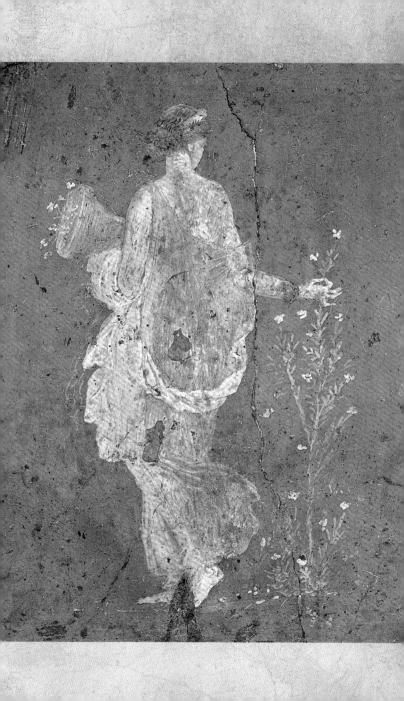

THE RACE FOR FAME

Many there are whose pleasure lies
In striving for the victor's prize,
Whom dust clouds, drifting o'er the throng
As whirls the Olympic car along,
And kindling wheels, and close shunned goal
Amid the highest gods enrol.

Branwell Brontë (1817-1848)

SUNT QUOS CURRICULO PULVEREM OLYMPICUM
COLLEGISSE IUVAT METAQUE FERVIDIS
EVITATA ROTIS PALMAQUE NOBILIS
TERRARUM DOMINOS EVEHIT AD DEOS.

Horace, *Odes 1.1, lines 3-6*

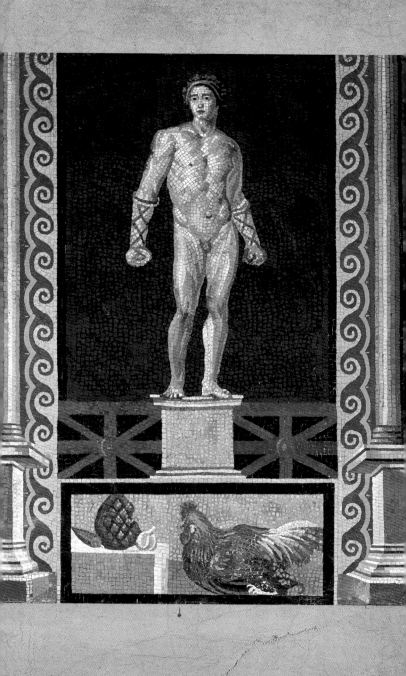

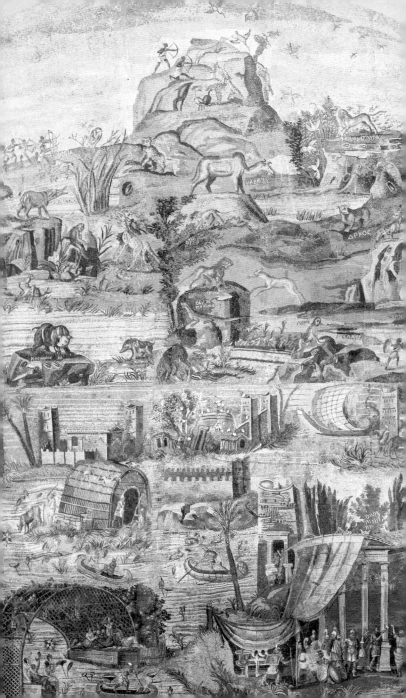

THE END OF THE FLOOD

When that this trump amid the sea
  was set to Triton's mouth,
He blew so loud that all the streams
  both east, west, north and south
Might easily hear him blow retreat,
  and all that heard the sound
Immediately began to ebb
  and draw within their bound.
Then 'gan the sea to have a shore,
  and brooks to find a bank,
And swelling streames of flowing floods
  within their channels sank.

Arthur Golding (*c.*1536-1606)

TUM QUOQUE, UT ORA MADIDA RORANTIA BARBA
CONTIGIT ET CECINIT IUSSOS INFLATA RECEPTUS,
OMNIBUS AUDITA EST TELLURIS ET AEQUORIS UNDIS,
ET QUIBUS EST UNDIS AUDITA, COERCUIT OMNES.
IAM MARE LITUS HABET, PLENOS CAPIT ALVEUS AMNES,
FLUMINA SUBSIDUNT COLLESQUE EXIRE VIDENTUR:
SURGIT HUMUS, CRESCUNT LOCA DECRESCENTIBUS UNDIS.

Ovid, *Metamorphoses 1, lines 339-345*

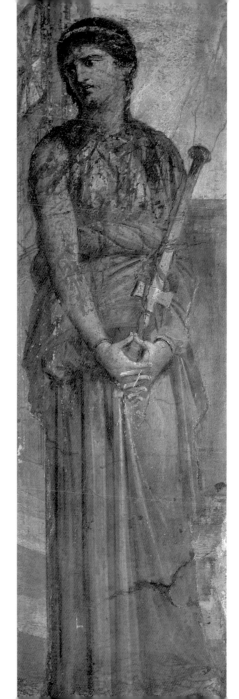

THE WITCHCRAFT OF MEDEA

By charms I raise and lay the winds,
   and burst the viper's jaw.
And from the bowels of the earth
   both stones and trees do draw.
Whole woods and forests I remove:
   I make the mountains shake,
And even the earth itself to groan
   and fearfully to quake.
I call up dead men from their graves:
   and thee O lightsome moon
I darken oft, though beaten brass
   abate thy peril soon.
Our sorcery dims the morning fair,
   and darks the sun at noon.

Arthur Golding (*c.*1536-1606)

VENTOS ABIGOQUE VOCOQUE.

VIPEREAS RUMPO VERBIS ET CARMINE FAUCES,

VIVAQUE SAXA SUA CONVULSAQUE ROBORA TERRA

ET SILVAS MOVEO IUBEOQUE TREMESCERE MONTIS

ET MUGIRE SOLUM MANESQUE EXIRE SEPULCRIS!

TE QUOQUE, LUNA, TRAHO, QUAMVIS TEMESAEA LABORES

AERA TUOS MINUANT: CURRUS QUOQUE CARMINE NOSTRO

PALLET AVI, PALLET NOSTRIS AURORA VENENIS!

Ovid, *Metamorphoses 7, lines 202-209*

DAYS OF WINE AND ROSES

They are not long, the weeping and the laughter,
    Love and desire and hate:
I think they have no portion in us after
    We pass the gate.

They are not long, the days of wine and roses:
    Out of a misty dream
Our path emerges for a while, then closes
    Within a dream.

Ernest Dowson (1867-1900)

VITAE SUMMA BREVIS SPEM NOS VETAT INCHOARE LONGAM.

Horace, *Odes 1.4, line 15*

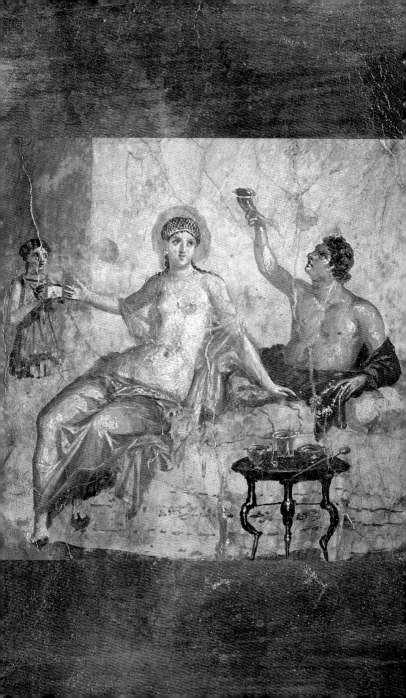

GIVE ME A THOUSAND KISSES

My Lesbia let us love and live,
And to the winds my Lesbia give
Each cold restraint, each boding fear
Of age and all her saws severe.

. . . .

Then come, with whom alone I live,
A thousand kisses take and give,
Another thousand – to the store
Add hundreds – then a thousand more.

William Wordsworth (1770-1850)

VIVAMUS, MEA LESBIA, ATQUE AMEMUS,
RUMORESQUE SENUM SEVERIORUM
OMNES UNIUS AESTIMEMUS ASSIS.

. . . .

DA MI BASIA MILLE, DEINDE CENTUM,
DEIN MILLE ALTERA, DEIN SECUNDA CENTUM,
DEINDE USQUE ALTERA MILLE, DEINDE CENTUM.

Catullus, *Poem 5, lines 1-3 and 7-9*

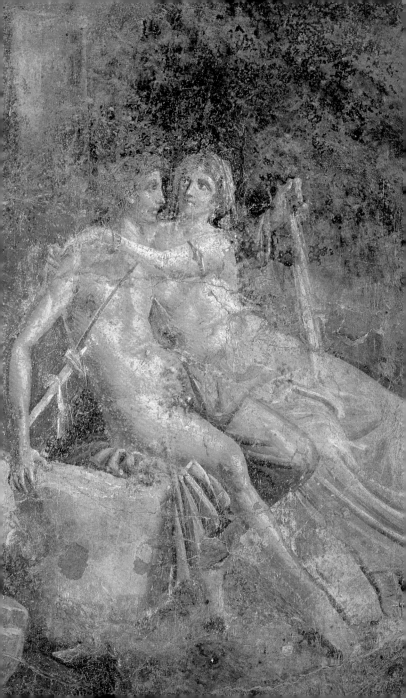

BIOGRAPHICAL NOTES ON THE POETS

GAIUS VALERIUS CATULLUS
∞ c. 84 - c. 54 BC

Catullus was born into a wealthy family living in the colonized Celtic settlement of Verona; his father was a close friend of Julius Caesar. At seventeen, Catullus went to live in Rome, where he moved in high society and became the leading member of a group of innovative poets. In 57 BC, he went to work in Asia Minor as an aide to the governor of Bithynia, returning home afterward lonely and penniless.

One of his best-known poems is "Hail and Farewell," the poignant epitaph he wrote for his elder brother, who died while Catullus was still in his twenties.

The great love of Catullus's life was Clodia, wife of the consul Quintus Metellus Celer. They met three years before her husband died. Of the 116 Catullan poems that survive, the most famous are the 25 addressed to Clodia (whose identity the poet concealed by calling her Lesbia), in which he records passions shifting from violent ecstasy to the deepest despair.

QUINTUS HORATIUS FLACCUS

∽ 65-8 BC

Born in Venusia, Horace was the son of a freed slave
(Flaccus, or "flap-eared," may have been his father's
name as a slave). He went to school in Rome and studied
philosophy in Athens. Later he fought with the
republican army under Brutus during the civil war and
returned to Rome to find most of his property
confiscated. With what he salvaged, he bought a
clerkship in the civil service and started to publish
his poems.

So original were his cool-voiced *Epodes* and early
Satires in portraying Roman society that he soon
attracted the notice of an influential patrician named
Maecenas, Minister for the Arts, who became his
patron. Horace eventually became Poet Laureate.

At his villa in Tivoli, outside Rome, he composed
many of his eighty-eight *Odes*, which have remained
one of the best-loved anthologies ever written.

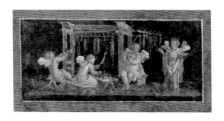

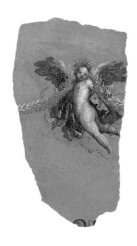

PUBLIUS OVIDIUS NASO
∞ 43 BC - AD 17

The name Naso ("Big-nose") probably refers to one of Ovid's ancestors. He was born into a distinguished family, educated in Rome, and afterward sent on a finishing tour of Greece and Asia Minor.

Ovid's first book, the *Amores*, achieved enormous success; so, too, did the *Ars amatoria,* a treatise on finding, winning, and enjoying love, which delighted many, but shocked others. He also wrote the *Heroides* and the *Fasti*. But most people remember him for the *Metamorphoses,* a collection of beautiful transformation myths, which he never completed.

When he was fifty, Ovid was accused of high treason and was banished from Rome at the same time as the emperor Augustus's granddaughter Julia. Their treason is thought to have been linked in some way with the *Ars amatoria.* Ovid was sent to a remote frontier post on the Romanian coast of the Black Sea, where he died in exile at the age of sixty.

PUBLIUS VERGILIUS MARO

∽ 70-19 BC

Born near Mantua in Cisalpine Gaul, Virgil grew up in a
farming family. He studied at Cremona and Milan,
completed his education in Rome, and later became one
of a group of court poets attached to Maecenas, Minister
for the Arts, and a friend of Horace.

In 41BC, Virgil's farmlands were among those
confiscated by the victorious triumvirs (Mark Antony,
Lepidus, and Octavian, the future Augustus) and
re-allocated to returning soldiers.

Against a background of civil war Virgil wrote the
Eclogues, describing an ideal pastoral landscape. The
success of the *Eclogues* made him a wealthy man and
enabled him to settle in Campania. There he poured his
knowledge of agriculture into the *Georgics,* whose
publication confirmed him as the leading poet of the
Augustan age. He spent the last eleven years of his life
composing the *Aeneid*, a poem in twelve books that tells
the epic story of Aeneas the Trojan, legendary founder
of the Roman nation.

At fifty, returning from a voyage to Greece, Virgil
died of a fever at Brundisium.

THE ART OF POMPEII AND HERCULANEUM

POMPEII AND HERCULANEUM were two small Italian towns buried in volcanic ash when Mount Vesuvius erupted in AD 79. Their rediscovery in the eighteenth century proved to be a landmark in the history of archaeology, and after nearly 250 years of continuous excavation they are now among the best-known sites of antiquity. The extraordinary circumstances of their burial, which resulted in the preservation of houses, furnishings, and, at Herculaneum, even organic materials such as food, have provided archaeologists and historians with an unparalleled opportunity to study life in late Republican and early Imperial Rome – the age of Catullus, Virgil, Horace, and Ovid.

Among the most important discoveries have been the wall-paintings and mosaic pavements that decorated the houses of the townspeople. Mosaics of the period were usually nonfigurative, often consisting of simple black-and-white geometric patterns; but excavations at Pompeii and Herculaneum have yielded some finely worked mosaic pictures based on Greek models. These pictures were usually set in the middle of a pavement, surrounded by ornamental borders or plain white chippings. Some were bought from studios; others were imported from Greece. Foremost among these is the stupendous Alexander mosaic, nearly six meters long by over three meters high, which reproduces a battle painting depicting a mass of struggling soldiers and plunging horses.

Wall-paintings have been found in almost every

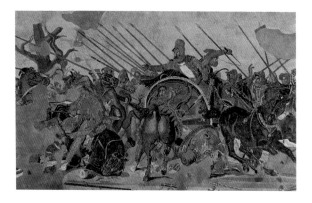

house at Pompeii and Herculaneum, however modest. No other society in human history seems to have lavished so much care on the ornamentation of its domestic environment. The wall-paintings were carried out on plaster in a fresco technique that required elaborate preparation. The most expensive decorations were applied in the most important rooms and contained architectural motifs to divide up the wall surface.

Experts divide Roman painting chronologically into four styles:

The First Style, fashionable in the second century BC, imitated masonry or veneers of colored marble, with the plaster worked in relief to suggest blockwork.

The Second Style (c. 80-c. 20BC) created an illusion of grand architecture, in which different layers and receding colonnades were suggested by the use of shading and perspective.

The Third Style, current in the age of Augustus (when Virgil, Horace, and Ovid were publishing their poems), introduced a mannered elegance in the form of matchstick columns and fantasy pavilions, accompanied by delicate polychrome ornament and broad areas of red, black, and pale blue.

The Fourth Style, introduced around the middle of the first century AD, retained the fantasy architecture but revived the use of recessive effects and introduced warm golden colors.

The decorations served as a framework for painted pictures, often based on Greek "old masters." Most highly prized were scenes from Greek mythology, but many other attractive works in genres such as still life and landscape have been unearthed.

Roger Ling

PROFESSOR OF CLASSICAL ART AND ARCHAEOLOGY
UNIVERSITY OF MANCHESTER

ORIGINAL SITES OF THE
FRESCOES AND MOSAICS, WHERE KNOWN

Pompeii: 5, 13, 14-15, 16, 22, 37, 39, endpapers; House of the Birds 56;
House of the Citharist 69; House of the Dioscuri 64; House of the Faun 75;
House of the Golden Cupids 31, 45; House of Siricus 11; House of the
Tragic Poet 21; House of the Vettii 19; Villa of the Mysteries 53; Exedra,
House (V, 1, 18) 32; House (VI, 17, 42) 54-55; House (VII, 2, 6) 48;
Castellammare di Stabia: Villa of Varanus 59;
Herculaneum: 27; **Sepphoris, Lower Galilee**: 24

Photographic Acknowledgments

*For permission to reproduce the frescoes and mosaics on the following pages and for
supplying photographs, the Publishers would like to thank:*
AKG London / Erich Lessing (National Museum of Archaeology, Naples):
5, 11, 14-15, 21, 22, 27, 32, 35, 37, 39, 64, 67, 69, 75, endpapers
© **The British Museum**: 29; **L'Erma di Bretschneider, Rome**: 54-55
The J. Paul Getty Museum: 40 (96.AG.172), 47 (70.AG.92), 71 (72.AG.82), 72 (73.AG.103)
The Hebrew University of Jerusalem, Institute of Archaeology: 24
Scala, Florence: 19, 31, 45, 53, 56; National Museum of Archaeology, Naples 9, 13,
16, 48, 50, 59, 61; Museo delle Terme, Rome 43; Museum of Archaeology, Palestrina 62

Acknowledgments

The Publishers would like to thank the following for permission to reprint copyright
material: the Estate of L.P. Wilkinson for the extract from Georgics of Virgil: Critical Survey
(Cambridge University Press, 1969); the Estate of Arthur Symons for his translation of
Poem 86, by Catullus.

First published in Great Britain in 1998 by Frances Lincoln Limited,
4 Torriano Mews, Torriano Avenue, London NW5 2RZ

Published in the United States of America by the J. Paul Getty Museum,
1200 Getty Center Drive, Los Angeles, California 90049-1687

All rights reserved

Cataloguing-in-Publication Data

A garden of Roman verse: poems of ancient Rome.
        p.   cm.
Poems of Catullus, Virgil, Horace, and Ovid with translations into English by various authors.
ISBN 0-89236-527-7
1. Latin poetry—Translations into English. 2. Latin poetry. 3. Rome—Poetry.
PA6164.G37   1998
        871'.0108—dc21   98—15862
                                CIP

EDITED BY YVONNE WHITEMAN
DESIGNED BY SARAH SLACK

Set in Perpetua and Trajan
Printed in Hong Kong
1 3 5 7 9 8 6 4 2

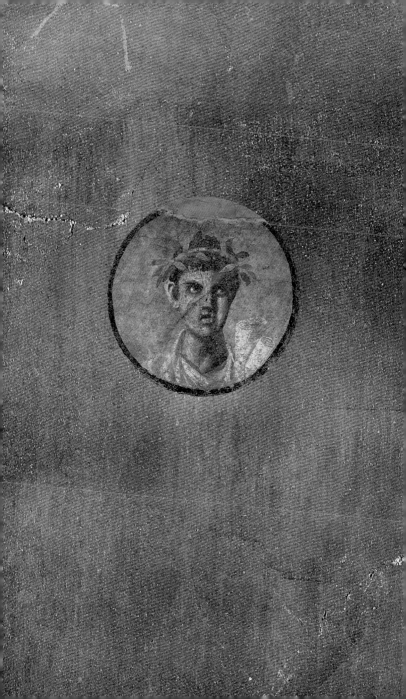